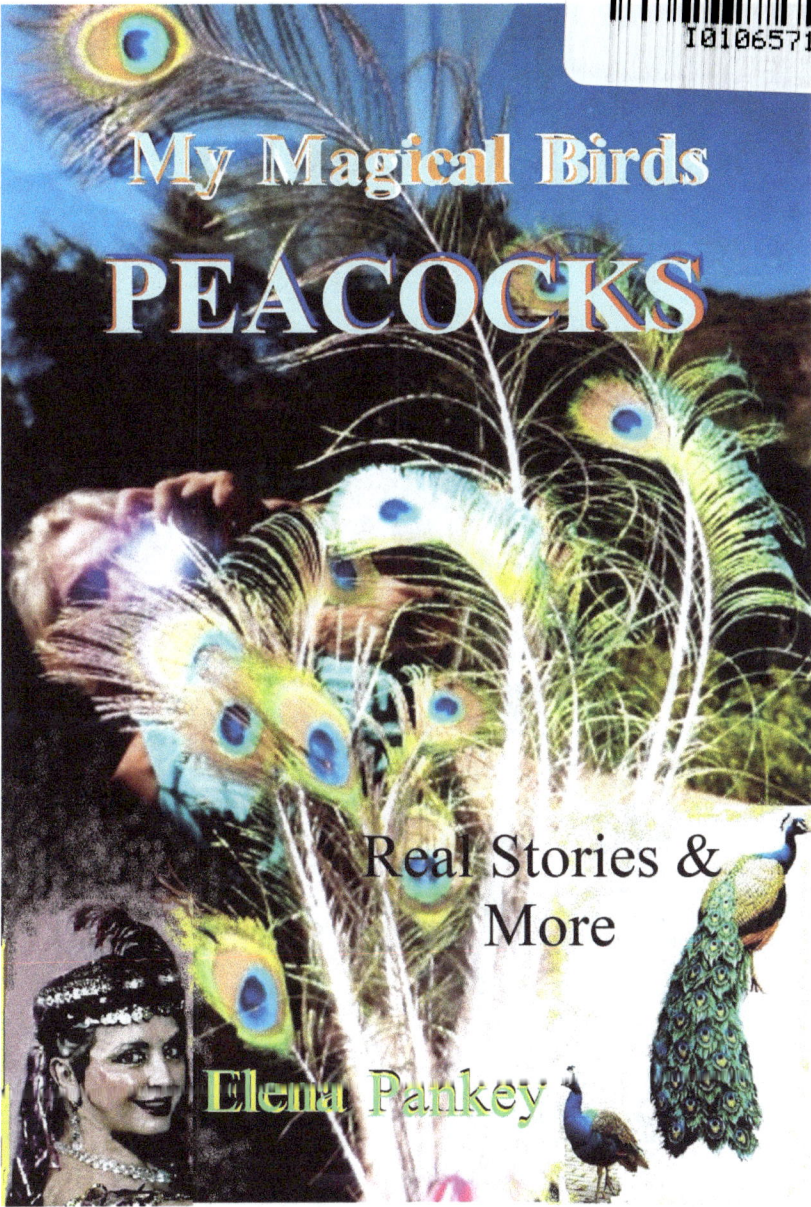

My Magical Birds

PEACOCKS

Real Stories & More

Elena Pankey

978-1-952907-85-2

My Magical Birds
Peacocks
Real Stories and More

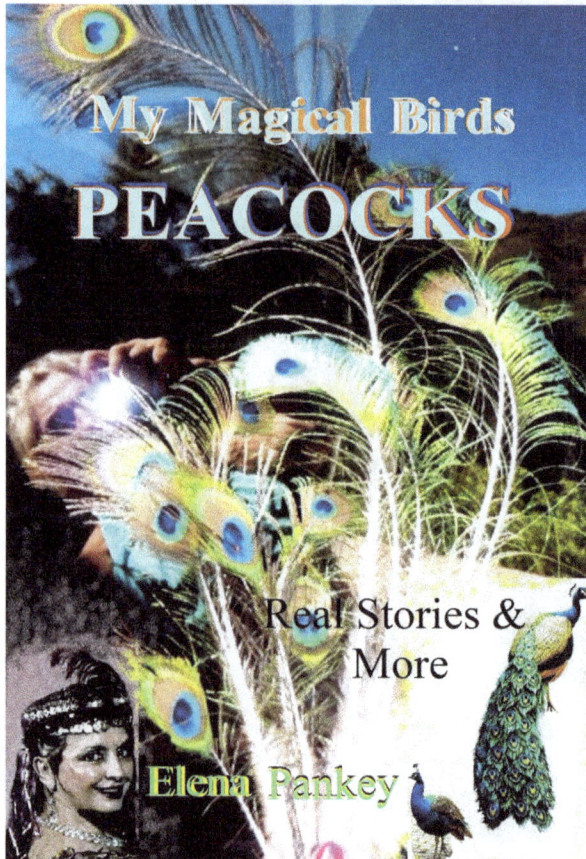

Elena Pankey

ISBN: 9781952907852

Contents

Introduction

The book contains real stories from the lives of two amazing birds - peacocks, who unexpectedly appeared on a California ranch. It also includes fascinating information and wonderful photographs taken by the author. The book contains poems, legends, riddles and clever proverbs about this "bird of paradise," as it was popularly called.

This wonderful book will bring a lot of joy, knowledge and emotional entertainment to both adults and children. The time you are spending together with your loved ones, as a family, while usefully learning something new, is the most precious thing in human relationships.

This book is a good gift for anyone and at any time of the year. Rejoice together in the wonders of the world and nature.

***

For many years our life at the isolated California ranch was safe, pleasant and quiet. Only one thing was to do: creating a beautiful garden on the empty wild slop, planting fruit trees, beautiful bushes and flowers. Also, it was good taking care for dogs and that was all our activities.

But a desire to be more active, to meet people and have more exiting life moved us to a dance world. We started to go out, learning ballroom and Argentine tango, organizing charity concerts, traveling and cruising.

Years passed, and it was time for something quieter. As it turned out, it was time for writing.

Then, the new time has come: an adventure with peacocks. This was a new, unusual and unknown world for us.

Part 1

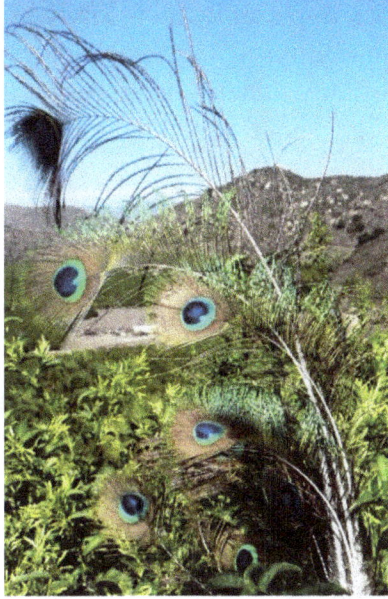

***

Miracle

"The fairy tale is a lie, but there is a hint in it - a lesson for good fellows." An old grandmother told to her granddaughter, trying to teach her some wisdom of ancient beliefs.

One morning there was a piercing cry of a large bird in the garden, as if she was calling someone. We have never heard such a strange and loud scream. The huge, ceiling to floor windows of the southern part of the house looked out towards the garden hill. Looking out the kitchen window, we were struck by the strange vision of a blue bird striding importantly through the garden, as if it already owned it.

To our deepest surprise, it was a beautiful Indian peacock, with very long colorful tail. These rainbow-colored feathers had special eye-shaped markings typical of this species of peacock.

Suddenly, seeing that I was approaching him, the peacock, apparently, wanted to make the best impression and show off his amazing beauty. He raised his tail up, spread it like a fan and shouted his greeting three times. The bird achieved an amazing effect, and we froze in surprise, not daring to scare him away.

How could such a "bird of paradise" get into the fenced garden of this ranch on a high hill, far from people and civilization?

The beautiful peacock importantly and slowly rejoiced at the huge space where he suddenly found himself, and pecked something on the ground. Then, he settled comfortably under a bush, rested a little, and again began to walk around the garden, shouting loudly and calling for at least someone to keep him company.

As it turned out, peacocks do not like to live alone. On their own, they become depressed and sad. In such case, they shout loudly inviting their friends to join them, calling their girlfriends to share their new paradise life. But most often their scream is a way to explain to people something about their needs.

This handsome peacock became not only a decoration for the garden. All day long he devoured all insects and lizards that were there in abundance. He had strong, sharp claws and could repel someone's aggression or whoever interfered with him. Sometimes he came very close to the house and nestled under the canopy where our old dog once lived. For some time he would sit there, looking to the horizon while remembering his former life in a cramped cage. Now he was finally happy, having found the whole garden to himself.

Soon, it became clear to us that someone at night brought him in a plastic bag and dropped it in our garden. That plastic bag was soon found near the trees.

At first, somebody was amazed by the beauty of this royal bird and wanted to own it without studying its characteristics. But peacocks need a lot of space and suffer while living in small cages or in a backyard. Also, during the mating season, the frequent heartbreaking scream of male peacocks causes quite natural displeasure among neighbors.

Peacocks scream very sharply. It is especially unpleasant to hear their "singing" at night. Apparently, the neighbors of the previous frivolous owners of the peacock were tired of his loud cries, and began to complain about the disturbance of their peace. And, wanting to get rid of this thoughtless purchase, the previous owners threw the bird out to our ranch while he was sleeping.

But this beautiful peacock seemed to suggest the need to shine, to show one's best side, and to please those who lived nearby with its beauty. It was interesting to watch the bird.

But again, one inconvenience soon began to interfere with our quiet life. The peacock obviously was very thirsty and hungry, and his scream was the only language of communication with which he tried to explain his needs to people. Also, it looked like he was very lonely, even in the beautiful large garden. It was time for him to start a family and to have some children. The most important, he wanted to have a safe shelter, asking us to build one for him.

But shocked by his sudden appearance in our place and not knowing anything about this big bird's habitat, we did not understand his constant, loud and sharp scream. He screamed a lot and it was irritating and nerve wracking…

***

***

With the appearance of the peacock in the garden, Allen began to read about these amazing birds. It turns out that they once lived on the Pacific islands, in India, and Australia. "Firebirds" were present in the stories of sailors who admired the bright plumage and beauty of the birds.

According to legend, the Dutch pioneers were the first to see the birds and named them "Birds of Paradise." Wonderful birds from legends and fairy tales have always attracted a lot of attention, and kings loved to breed them.

It is interesting that the peacock embodies the symbol of radiant glory, immortality, greatness and incorruptibility. But at the same time, it is also a symbol of pride and vanity. In the ancient cultures of India and later Iran, the magnificent tail of the peacock became a symbol of the all-seeing Sun and the eternal cosmic cycles.

***

Loss

The peacock walked carefree and importantly in the garden.
P periodically he was spreading his wonderful tail like a fan. When I
began slowly approaching him, he demonstrated his unearthly beauty,
and was shouting about the futility of a dull existence where there is no
concern for beauty.

Later in the day, somehow, unexpectedly, dogs jumped out into the
garden. Young Tuzik had a strong intuition and sense of a hunter. When
he saw the peacock, he wanted only to catch it. And with an exciting yell,
he rushed after the bird.

The peacock was very frightened and ran away, as fast as he could.
Then, he quickly took off, having flown a little, and sat down on a
spreading oak tree at the bottom of the road, far from the garden. He was
sitting there, trumpeting menacingly and loudly, in a low voice timbre,
exactly like an elephant would do.

The old dog Sonya stood nearby, silently marveling at all this energetic
and unusual activity in her quiet garden. The loud barking of Tuzik at a
defenseless bird sitting high in a tree seemed especially unnecessary to
her. After looking a little more at all this needless fuss, she left. And I had
to take Tuzik to another part of the yard, away from the garden.

It was getting dark. Usually after sunset, peacocks try to quickly find
a comfortable and safe place to spend the night. But this young peacock
apparently forgot that he can fly. Also, without flying it was difficult to
get back into the fenced garden, far away from the tree where the bird was
sitting. It was dangerous to climb down from the tree, but he still tried to
find his way "home" on foot.

And suddenly a piercingly loud cry of a peacock for help echoed
throughout the surrounding area of the ranch. It was a pack of coyotes
making their way to the oak tree under which the bird was sitting.

Feeling Guilty

The next day, Allen, the lady of the house and her dogs went to look for the peacock. But near the oak tree where he was sitting the night before, the dogs became agitated and ran around it, sniffing the ground. Then, they saw that the most beautiful bluish-green feathers from the tail of a magical bird were scattered everywhere. This is all that remains of the handsome peacock after meeting with a flock of coyotes.

Feeling guilty, Allen collected the beautiful feathers, brought them home and placed them in a vase. In the corner of a refrigerator, they stood tall, like a memory, or like an urn containing the ashes of someone dear to you who had died, and whom we had not taken care of while he was alive. But those dead feathers were only a dim reflection of the unearthly beauty that the peacock showed in the garden.

For some most intelligent and sensitive people, the feeling of guilt often torments conscience, as if it "eats" a person.

Allen wanted to believe that maybe one morning this bird of paradise will miraculously appear in the garden again, waking everybody up with a special cry calling for a friend and love. She so wanted to believe in miracles or create miracles herself. And this is how she set off on a journey to find the bird of paradise and return it to the now dim and so empty garden...

***

Part 11

***

Cages

Allen once learned that peacocks have very sensitive sleep, and no one can sneak into the garden without waking them up. The peacock will begin to scream loudly, calling everyone for help, if they sense strangers or danger. So, it turned out that this amazing bird could become an excellent protective bell for the garden. So, Allen and her husband Victusha decided to buy two young peacocks.

But first it was good to get ready and to prepare everything necessary for the new residents of the ranch. It was important that they could live safely and joyfully without too much screaming.

The workers were hired to build huge cages on the slop of the garden. Each cage was made of wood and covered with iron mesh.

For a safety at night, the wild peacocks always fly high into a tree and rest there. This was the main thing in the construction of the cages for amazing birds. The cages were built quite spacious and very tall, having several shelves for birds to rest and roost at night.

The cages also had to be wide enough for the peacocks to open their tails and show them off. Moreover, all three cages were connected and the birds could walk wherever they wanted. This passage with fifteen steps led upstairs to the garden. And then, it was also covered with wire mesh, so that none of the predators - the peacock's enemies - (like a hungry raccoon, for example) could get inside the cages.

Soon all three huge cages were made.

10

***

New Place

After building the first cage at the end of May, Allen found a local peacock farm with a good reputation and purchased two young birds. They were the most beautiful, colorful birds named "Indian Blue". Moreover, the peacocks were three year old brothers who had never been separated before. That's why they were sold together.

The owner of the peacocks arrived with her husband, bringing huge birds wrapped in plastic bags and with their wings tied. Only their heads stuck out to make it easier for them to breathe.

We led everyone into the newly built first cage, and the owner untied the bags. The first peacock Peter immediately shook himself and flew higher onto the shelf and away from everyone.

But his two minutes younger brother Petrusha, already untied, sat quietly, motionless. It was clear that they were both very scared about the move and the new place.

Also, they were sad to leave the large family of chickens on the previous farm. Peter was especially outraged by the fact that no one asked him for that resettlement, that nobody took into account his opinion about moving to a new place.

"*Nobody respects the rights of birds anymore,*" he muttered, white sitting up in the new home.

Soon after, their former owners got ready to go home. Suddenly, the peacocks heard the sound of their car driving away, that familiar to them dear car sound disappearing away…. They turned their heads with longing

11

towards the receding sound, and loudly, with a tearing-sharp scream they shouted after it:

"What about us!? Take us back with you! We want to go home!!"

It looked as if the peacocks knew that they were left in this new and foreign place forever...

***

Safe House

After a few days in the new place, the peacocks seemed to become happier with their wonderful new home. In these huge cages, with well-fortified lower walls, they felt safe.

The brothers spent the entire day in one of the cages on the ground, moving very little. Gradually they got used to the new environment and stopped screaming. Only occasionally did they react to some sounds in the garden or to a squirrel that came to visit them without permission.

They had special voices for different events. Peacocks especially often used the elephant's trumpet voice when they were trying to appear important and frightening to predators. They used it when they were unpleased with the fact that they were sent out to a walk.

Twice a day the new owner entered the cage to clean it. In this case, she took a fluffy twig from a pine tree and sent the peacocks outside. She wanted the peacocks to walk in the garden, eat fresh grass, and look for items useful for them like protein worms or something else. She tried to convince them that it would be useful for them to be outside of their cages.

But the peacocks did not believe in this, and screamed loudly in indignation, not wanting to go out for a walk. After an enforced push out, they stood near the door leading to their kingdom for five minutes. But seeing that their cherished door to the safe place was closed, they began to wander up and down along the mesh surrounding the cages and shouted:

"We are Peacock! Open the cage, please! The peacock is better off at home! A peacock at home will live up to fifty years with good feeding! Let us in!"

They were shouting it until the new owner would come and let them in.

After watching such a scene several times, the new owner realized that

her birds preferred to be inside, in the safety of their home. They did not want to walk in such tempting but treacherous freedom. Especially they stopped to go out after they saw the irrigation line working, got slightly wet, and then heard the dogs barking nearby, very close to them…

They did not want to graze on their own looking for some food outside, pecking something there. In such case, the bird owner had to collect some fresh healthy grass called "sedge" for them every day, and bring it inside to their home.

Therefore, their free "walk wondering" was reduced to five minutes while she cleaned the cages. And then the peacocks rushed back, hid in the corner by the mirror and sat there all day.

In the first several days and nights after the arriving, they sadly meowed, exactly like a real cat would complain about something. It's amazing that birds once learned to imitate elephant or a cat using their own voice. But it sounded very pitiful, as if the peacocks were yearning for their former home, where they lived for their first three years.

At night, the peacocks flew up to a high shelf and slept until the morning, hiding their heads under their wings or putting it on their chest. While one was in a deep sleep, his brother was on duty, observing everything around him, and periodically shouted if something bothered him.

- *"The peacocks are the tenants here! Everything is booked and occupied here! Stay away"*

The Dogs

Some time ago, Allen noticed that someone was secretly wandering

around the house and in her beautiful garden that she was creating and cared for many years. One day the fresh flowers suddenly began to dry up and flowering bushes began to die. Another day, many fruit trees and all the young cypresses near the walls of the house suddenly turned completely black and dried up. The plants clearly showed all the signs that they had been sprayed with a special poison.

And then one day a terrible tragedy happened. Those hired criminals poisoned a devoted big dog that courageously defended the garden from their invasion. The owners took him to the hospital, and for seven days there the veterinarians fought for his life. The old dog, even realizing that he was dying, defended his owners until the last minute...

His longtime friend, the other German shepherd Sonya, witnessed the death of her precious friend. After that tragedy, the impressionable and affectionate Sonia, afraid of attracting the attention of strangers, stopped barking altogether.

That same year 2021, fleeing the bitterness of loss, the owner took home a new puppy. And a young dog also named Tuzik knew no fear and barked loudly, sensing enemies stealing avocados somewhere nearby.

Fearing for the lives of her dogs, Allen did not want to leave them in the yard overnight. Old Sonia and young Tuzik slept in the house, in their own special rooms.

The young boy Tuzik was not only jealous but also possessive. He believed that everything around him belonged only to him. Since childhood, accustomed to his mistress taking him everywhere in her car, he did not like to be alone in the yard. And when old Sonia stayed with him, he often growled at her, because she tried to lie closer to the front door or to the bowl of milk. Therefore, Sonia preferred to be in her former, quiet place in the garden, on the other side of the house.

One day, smart Sonia suddenly discovered with a surprise that someone was living in a large cage in her garden. The curious dog decided that it would be fun for her to get closer to the cages and watch the birds. She walked there quietly, like everything she did. Then she sat down not far away, and, looking at the peacocks, wondered about their strange loud cries. Sometimes she even asked them if there was anything she could do to help them feel more comfortable and safer.

Peacocks were very fearful birds, and they were especially afraid of dogs. So, Sonia's presence next to their cage made them very nervous. They looked around and huddled closer to the back of the cage.

Sometimes, when Allen was working in the garden, Tuzik would remain on the other side of the house. But he felt abandoned there, and barked restlessly and loudly, asking to take him closer to her and to the birds. The emotional Tuzik never forgot his greatest fun when he cheerfully tried to catch the first peacock in the garden.

Tuzik generally tried all the time to comprehend his purpose and the meaning of his life. And later, he felt that his job was to protect the mistress from her visit to the peacocks. He was especially worried and barked a lot at the birds when she called them "beautiful boys." The young Tuzik adored his mistress, and always wanted to be her only "beloved and beautiful boy."

***

Mirrors

At the beginning, Allen did not know anything about the life of the amazing peacock. And the builders, trying to please the owner, laid green artificial turf on the ground of the cage. The birds said nothing and began to get used to this new surface. Sometimes they even tried to dance around, slowly retreating back. Other times, they flew up to the top shelves and looked at what was happening outside.

However, the cages needed to be cleaned regularly, and cleaning up such artificial grass on the ground was difficult. This coating remained wet, dirty and began smelling strongly and badly. So one day the owner removed it and the birds felt much more comfortable on the ground with nothing on it. There on the dirt they spent most of their time burying themselves in the dust, like taking a bath.

Another time, the owner decided to "improve" the earthen surface and brought in small wooden flooring. But the peacocks were very unhappy about this. They were generally conservatives and did not like changes in their lives. Also, they were just simply frightened by this new flooring. They walked around it, or flew from one shelf to the other, avoiding the new floor. So the owner, observing it, decided to remove it as well, to make birds peaceful.

The security cameras inside the cages helped to watch the birds any time of the day. The peacock Peter loved most of all standing near a large mirror near the wall and admiring his tail. Sometimes he pecked something from the mirror. Seeing this, the owner bought several other mirrors and placed them in different cages. This way the youngest, quiet Petrusha could admire his plumage, as well, but in his own space, without crowding his brother.

Peacocks especially liked when their cages were cleaned and had new hay on the floor. The birds immediately would go to a clean area, and happily plop down on the fresh, cool earth near the mirrors. Peacocks often proudly walk around mirrors, turning around and admiring their amazing colorful tails.

***

Throughout the summer the peacocks were losing feather after feather and stopped "dancing" in front of the mirror. They even seemed to breathe better in the heat without them. It felt to them that it was now with a short tail even easier to jump between the shelves.

Their huge iridescent tails slowly fell off, decorating the floor of the cages with magical feathers. The hostess collected all this beauty and gave bouquets of feathers to all her friends and acquaintances.

Peacocks liked it and told her:

"Please, give our beauty out to everyone around. Whatever you give to others will be returned to you double. And we will grow our feathers for you again, and in the winter we will have long, beautiful tail for everyone's joy."

***

Characters

Since the introduction of Indian blue peacocks to the ranch, we have placed surveillance cameras in their cages and have learned a lot about the birds. The two peacocks, three-year-old brothers, were very close to each other and did everything together. These beautiful creatures were generally very gentle birds, with great character. Although at first glance they seemed lazy and slow, but at the same time, peacocks were observant and understood a lot.

One of them, Peter, is a few minutes older than his brother. This is why he keeps younger one as a subordinate, considering that he was wiser and in charge. It looked that Peter had the right of seniority, and felt that his little brother must obey him in everything. In this case, Peter was the one who approach the food first and choose the best of it. Meanwhile, Petrusha submissively waited on the sidelines until his brother had eaten enough.

Peter and Petrusha are grateful birds and always say "thank you" for everything their owner does for them. In their language, "thank you" sounds like a very quiet "Q." It sounds just like how regular yellow chickens sometimes cluck or mutter.

The most amazing thing is that they speak to each other in a special language. It is a gentle and quiet language of love and respect of theses mysterious birds. But this language is not open to everyone. Love must live in the heart in order to understand the language of living beings.

After the owner brings their favorite food (fresh blueberries, for example), they gently whisper to her *"Kui! - Thank you."*

Moreover, they are very polite to each other as well. Besides, they walk everywhere together, without overtaking the space of the other peacock in the front. Even when they were hurried by the owner to get out of the cages, they still were walking forward slowly and pleasantly, without pushing each other.

If one has gone somewhere a little further than the other, then his brother loudly notifies the straggler, advising him what to do and where to go. They constantly communicate, talking to each other in their quiet nice voice. But the elder Peter loves to give his suggestions that sound like a command. He imposes his opinion and controls his brother with the desire to help and support. He gets worried if he doesn't see his brother next to him and calls him loudly.

- *"Peacock Petrusha! Come here, I don't see you!"*

- *"There is delicious grass here,"* the lagging brother answers him, continuing to peck something in the grass and dreaming of less patronage.

"What a wonderful life we have here on the ranch, isn't it?!" - they soon started to whisper to each other, getting better accustomed to the new surrounding and new life style...

*** *

Unexpected Guest

Every evening the owner came to the cages to clean them and spray them with a special solution to remove germs. Also, Allen put new food in one of the cages in the morning and in the evening. She wanted the peacocks to be healthy, well-groomed, and to sleep well.

Somehow the little birds from the garden realized that they could also eat well and without any problems inside the peacocks' cages. They just had to try to get there somehow.

One day the first of these clever little birds finally found a fairly large space in the nets covering the roof. She rushed inside, quickly found food and had a good lunch. But then, she completely forgot how she got there, and how to get out now.

Then, seeing the coming owner, the bird got scared and began to rush around, trying to escape into the garden. But in this bustle and fear, she could not figure anything out, and fell between two different metal meshes covering the walls of the cells. She got stuck there and floundered, loudly screaming for salvation. The owner tried to help her and began waving a twig towards the door. But the bird was even more frightened, unable to reason logically. Then, she simply sat down on the crossbar and sat there silently, resting from the worries she had experienced.

Soon the beautiful peacocks swam smoothly and importantly into the main cage, preparing for the night snack and sleep. But then they saw a bird sitting on their favorite sleeping place. The peacocks simultaneously with a surprise turned their beautiful heads with the crowns towards Allen, and said:

-"*Did you rent out a corner to this new bird without asking our desire and permission*? –the older peacock Peter began to grumble out of a habit and the slightly indignant.

-"*She has been here before and ate our best grains! So, now you've decided to settle her here?* - echoed his brother Petrusha, who always followed or mimicked his older brother in everything.

-"*No, no,*" said the hostess, "*I just couldn't better help her find a way*

19

out."

- *"Well, it's a very simple thing to do,"* - answered Peter.

He immediately whispered something quietly to the garden guest, and amazingly, the poor bird quickly disappeared away in the correct direction. And the peacocks flew up to their shelves and remained there to rest until the morning.

***

Aggressive Coyote

In the wild, peacocks have many enemies, and between them, coyotes and raccoons were especially dangerous. One day, on video cameras, we saw a young coyote sneak into the garden at night. He walked back and forth near the cages, carefully examining the peacocks, and thinking about how to get inside. He had been hungry for a long time and dreamed of eating a tasty bird. The birds were very scared, screamed a lot, tried to jump higher, and even broke several feathers.

Despite the night time, the hostess Allen, hearing this noise, called her devoted dog Tuzik and ran out into the garden. But there she only heard someone's loud whistle, calling away the coyotes, and the noise of running feet.

***

Sassy Squirrel

One day, Petrusha decided to become more independent and went for a walk alone "to see the world." He boldly climbed all fifteen steps up and saw that the door to the tempting world of the garden was open. He courageously walked towards the exit, and through the bars connecting the cage to the garden, looked around the alluring area.

He stood on the last stairs for a while, wondering whether he should continue this journey alone. Then he carefully glanced further out.

Everything in the garden looked so green and inviting, much better than in the cages with bare soil. He walked a little near the cage, collecting something tasty in the grass. It was the highest pleasure to enjoy new surroundings and freedom that he had never had before. Petrusha felt so good that he even wanted to sing a little, and he cooed his quiet *"Kju-Kju."*

Then the peacock walked further and saw a trap with a squirrel inside it. Petrusha happily stopped near the cage and began to scold the squirrel. He shouted that these cheeky squirrels were generally "running amok" in the

20

garden, climbing into the peacocks' cages without any shame or conscience

And most importantly, just recently, this squirrel with its cubs, having climbed inside the peacocks' cage, jumped onto a hanging basket with delicious food and quickly ate it all.

The peacocks did not want to share their food with anyone. More often than not, they did not want to eat old food that had been touched by a squirrel's nose. Every night the brothers asked Allen to bring them something new, and especially loved dry dog food.

One day that squirrel with her little babies got inside the cage again. They were running there one after another, playing catching up and tasting the peacock's food. Then, their mother quickly climbed up the pole, found a small gap in the mesh, and all of them disappeared into the garden.

At that time the peacocks only had to pretend that they did not notice the squirrels' scampering, but still they remembered their pranks. And now the hour of reckoning has come: the squirrel is caught in a trap!

Walking in the garden, Petrusha suddenly saw the same squirrel and counted it out for its past tricks. Then he looked back, wishing to share his adventure and lucky discovery with his brother, but he did not see him. Petrusha got scared and began blowing his whistle at the top of his lungs.

-"*Brother, where are you, help me, how to get home?*"

His brother Peter immediately shouted where Petrusha should go, directing his brother back into the cage by his sharp and loud voice.

They were happy to meet again inside their safe home, where delicious seeds were waiting for them.

After eating and sitting comfortably close to each other, they began to clean their feathers. They spent quite a long time doing this activity. Having thoroughly cleaned themselves, the peacocks settled down on the ground next to the hanging plates with the remaining food, as if protecting it from future visits of the fat squirrel.

Then, the brothers exchanged thoughts about a wonderful day they had while sitting together in front of two mirrors, admiring their beauty, friendship and harmony. They were sure that to be completely happy they should always do something together and have fun. This was the most important thing in life.

***

Incident

Recently a strange incident happened. One day, Allen planned to go the beach house. She left some food for the birds inside the cage, locked the cages and went to the ocean. Two dogs always remained in the yard near the house during the absence of their owners. When the owner returned to the ranch at lunchtime, the older dog Sonia was taken back to the garden. There, in the shade of a spreading oak tree under a canopy, she usually spent the hot hours of the day.

Confident that the peacocks were inside their cages, the owner hurried into the house. But literally a minute later she heard the heart-rending cry of peacocks calling for help. Rushing into the garden, Allen saw in a shock that one of the peacocks was sitting high on the net that covered their cages. He was screaming in horror.

It was dog Sonia chasing the peacocks and drove one up there. And now Sonia was sitting nearby, watched with curiosity what would happen next. For a long time, the owner tried to help the peacock go down. But he was very frightened to find himself in the garden with the dog running after him. He flew up and again forgot how he could return home. Then Allen came close and simply pushed him down, thinking that he would fly into the cage. But the peacock after such untender touch became even more frightened, and loudly flapped its wings in despair.

- *Guard! What violence, trampling on the rights of peacocks*! - *save yourself, whoever can*! – he shouted in a panic and rushed to the other side of the garden, losing his feathers.

Allen spent a long time trying to persuade the peacock not to be afraid of her. But only after some time she finally managed to direct the bird towards the cage. Once safe, Peter looked around, looking for his brother, but he was nowhere to be found.

There were only a few tall trees in the garden where the peacock could hide. The hostess quickly looked up at them, and in desperation began to lookout for the other peacock. She thought that someone might have stolen the peacock or that it might have flown to the mountains that were nearby. Then she shouted to the surviving peacock, which was already in the cage:

-"*Help me to find Petrusha! - Call your brother*!"

And the peacock seemed to really understand that she needed his help. Peter began to loudly call his brother:

- "Peacock - Peacock! Where are you! Go home!" –
***

And at the time, when Sonia began her adventure, the other peacock flew in panic, fleeing from the dog that was hunting him. He got into the big oak tree over the road, and was sitting high there looking around.

It was clear that Petrusha was in great fright. Opening his beak, he breathed heavily and looked around, not knowing what to do. It was already evening, and the peacock was terribly thirsty and hungry. He had spent almost the entire day on the tree.

Having walked around all the surroundings, only at sunset, Allen finally saw the blue plumage of a peacock in the distance on a tall oak tree. Her joy knew no end. But, not wanting this magical bird to repeat the fate of the first peacock, the owner went to the oak tree to save him.

Coming very close to the tree, Allen tenderly asked him to come down. For a long time, she was standing under the tree, while begging her peacock not to walk back home, but to simply fly back.

At the same time, his brother worriedly called Petrusha, pointing in the right direction with his voice.

But, as it turned out later, peacocks fly only in critical cases, in fear, to escape something. So, poor Petrusha, in terrible fright from the dog hunting him, flew over a huge space. And then, still in shock from the experience, he completely forgot how to do it at all, and did not want to remember that he could fly. But only his flight could be the easiest and safest way to return home.

In the end, not knowing any other way, Petrusha slowly began to slide down the branches of the tree. The owner sighed with relief when he was on the ground. Having opened the gate to the fenced garden in advance, she slowly walked towards the bird, trying not to frighten him even more. Stopping a few steps away from him, Allen blocked his movement towards the mountains, and, waving a twig, directed him to the garden gate.

The peacock understood the desire of the loving mistress to help him, but did not show it. The proud bird simply slowly and majestically went up the hill, as if on a new walk. And the path back up to their cages was long and difficult, and led over several hills and through bushes.

But the peacock walked slowly and importantly, pecking something

23

along the way. But finally, to the great joy of his brother, they reached the cage.

Petrusha remembered this terrible adventure and how his owner saved him, and was very grateful. Later on, he often expressed his love and truest towards Allen. He knew that it is the most important thing for people and birds to be forever grateful for one for doing good things.

***

Later, after scrolling through the video recordings of the space around the cages, Allen saw that the peacocks walked for a long time near the cages. They pecked something on the ground, enjoying the wonderful weather and long-awaited freedom. Then they wanted to return home, but the cage door was closed.

Then the peacocks settled down comfortably near the closed door and began to wait for their mistress. But then suddenly the dog Sonia rushed in and started chasing the birds. So they found themselves at the saving height of the trees.

It's good that everything ends well. But everyone had a lot of worries and excitement from this strange incident.

Also, it was another leaning experience, as all life is only one leaning step after the other towards the wisdom....

***

Hawk

For some time, the owner, knowing that the peacocks would not fly away and could walk freely in the garden, kept the door to their cage open. But after the dangerous adventure in the garden, they did not often go out there for a walk.

However, always adventurous, the peacock Petrusha sometimes very carefully approached the gate leading outside. He sat at the threshold, observing what was so good in the wild, where everyone was so persistently striving.

At the same time, he often heard the voice of a screaming hawk very close by. The voice was frightening and thirsty for profit. This terrible voice of a ruthless predator sounded as if the hawk was hunting such naive simpletons as peacocks or owls were. Just for having fun, the hawk simply bit their twirling necks.

Having an excellent intuition and a sense of danger, Peacock Petrusha, having sat on the threshold to such a desired but dangerous freedom, soon returned to his more cautious brother. His brother now always watched him from afar, sitting in a huge and safe cage.

But still, occasionally, after sunrise and sunset, both peacocks went outside to look for something new. They tried to stay close to the cage gates. After walking outside for a little while and pecking at something on the ground, they called each other home, trumpeting like elephants. This trumpet sound was their main way of communication and sounded like a warning in case of danger.

Once, while reviewing the video from surveillance cameras, Allen, to her horror, saw how a hawk flew at full speed into the open cage of the peacocks.

He hunted for the small birds who sought salvation in the cages. Suddenly the hawk realized that in a fit of hunting, he was trapped in a narrow and closed space. He turned his head back, seeing that the cage gate was about to close and he would be trapped. The hawk was careful, smart and very quick in thinking. He immediately turned around and flew away.

Two small birds, sparrows, once inside the cages, could not find a way out, and fought there, entangled in the wire of double nets. And the peacocks, watching the desperate attempts of the little birds, whispered to them where the exit to freedom was. Peacocks generally considered themselves creatures of the highest order, royal birds, but they were kind to everyone around them.

"The cage doors will now always be closed to my beautiful peacocks. Or I'll have to sit nearby and watch what's happening in the garden while they are walking around, -" thought Allen.

After that new adventure, Allen did not leave the door opened. Every time she walked the dogs, Allen collected fresh grass (sage), which peacocks loved so much, and brought it to their cage. Sometimes to give her birds some fun, she cut a few apple tree branches and put them in the cage. Peacocks enjoyed eating these leaves; as well they loved mint leaves to complete their vitamins and nutrition.

***

The lives of peacocks were going on with many more daily adventures and stories…They generously provided interesting experience of care and love for their owner Allen, who was willing to learn from them how to live better in a captivity… But it is a different story for a new book

***

Poem

Beneath the sky of blue the golden city stands with crystal-clear lucent gates and with a star ablaze. The garden lies within it blossoms far and wide. The beasts of stunning beauty are roaming inside. There is a lion with a fiery-yellow mane, and the blue calf has eyes so deep and bright. There is the golden eagle from the heavens, whose eternal gaze's so unforgettable…And from that sky of blue the star is shining through. This star is yours, oh angel mine. It always shined for you. Who loved is beloved. Who giveth light is blessed. So go after the light of guiding star into this awesome land. The fiery lion will meet you at the gate; and the blue calf with eyes so deep and bright. And the golden eagle from the heavens, whose eternal gaze's so unforgettable…

***

Interesting to Know…

"Proud as a peacock" is a saying that is used to mean a vain or self-centered person. The phrase comes from the plumage of the male peafowl (females are peahens). When a male is courting, he spreads his tail feathers, sometimes five feet in length, out in a fan pattern to attract a female.

***

The ancient Greeks believed that the flesh of the peacock never decayed, even after death, and so it became a symbol of immortality.

26

Early Christians adopted the symbolism and the peacock thus became an emblem of the Resurrection and the eternal life of Christ.

***

The Peacock

His loud sharp call seems to come from nowhere. Then, a flash of turquoise is in the papal tree (*Sacred fig*). The slender neck arched away from you as he descends, and as he darts away, a glimpse of the very end of his tail. I was told that you have to sit in the veranda and read a book, preferably one of your favorites, with great concentration. The moment you begin to live inside the book a blue shadow will fall over you.

The wind will change direction. The steady hum of bees in the bushes nearby will stop. The cat will awaken and stretch. Something has broken your attention. And if you look up in time you might see the peacock turning away as he gathers his tail to shut those dark glowing eyes, violet fringed with golden amber. It is the tail that has to blink for eyes that are always open.

***

I Saw a Peacock

I Saw a Peacock, with a fiery tail,
I saw a Blazing Comet, drop down hail,
I saw a Cloud, with Ivy circled round,
I saw a sturdy Oak, creep on the ground,
I saw a Pismire (ant), swallow up a Whale,
I saw a raging Sea, brim full of Ale,

I saw a Venice Glass, Sixteen foot deep,
I saw a well, full of men's tears that weep,
I saw their eyes, all in a flame of fire,
I saw a House, as big as the Moon and higher,
I saw the Sun, even in the midst of night,
I saw the man that saw this wondrous sight.

***

King Solomon and Peacock

I heard that once upon a time a peacock came to King Solomon, heading a delegation of feathery folks. He was ostensibly displaying its plumes, showing off its flashy garments. Alternately, revealing and concealing its bright feathers. He said to the King: "I have a case I wish to present before you. I think it is time, your majesty, you looked into it. That's why, my Lord, I came here at your doorsteps. Am I not the meadows incarnate; with all their blossoms and sparkling lights? Haven't I gathered in my person every form of beauty, every shade and hue of color? Here I am, the Master of all birds at your door! Must I be left without what I most eagerly desire?

When I am of noble lineage and decent descent?

Alas, here I am, deprived of a melodious voice! I have never been able to enchant the hearts with my sweet tuneful strains, nor do I entertain the ears with my songs. Behold, the littlest of birds is capable of inflaming the passions of lovers. Yea, even kings sway when a singing bird warbles, swaying on its branch."

King Solomon answered, saying: "Thus has it been ordained! Great is God's wisdom, wonderful are His handiwork. Indeed, you are self-conceited! Nor are you content with what God has created. You call yourself the king of birds, yet are lacking in wisdom and understanding. Well, dear peacock, had you a beautiful voice, You would be even haughtier, Moreover, you would not deign to talk to anyone"...(A. Shawqi)

***

About Author

Elena Pankey has more than 45 years of job experience in different areas. During many years she devoted her life to dancing, performing and producing charity shows. Elena is an Argentine Tango Master, and people called her "Twinkles Feet", "Queen of Tango," "Tango Icon". After finishing her dancing, Elena began to write different life stories. She is the author of many fun books on different subjects, including fun fairy tales, children's books, about dogs and cats, about Argentine Tango dancing, art, and adventures. While living in CA, she continues to travel the world, teaching, dancing and writing.

***

Ecclesiastes 3: 1-8

"To everything, there is a season, and a time to every purpose under the heaven: A time to be born, and a time to die; a time to plant, and a time to pluck up that which is planted.
A time to kill, and a time to heal; a time to break down and a time to build up. A time to weep, and a time to laugh; a time to mourn and a time to dance.
A time to cast away stones and a time to gather stones together, a time to embrace, and a time to refrain from embracing. A time to get, and a time to lose; a time to keep, and a time to cast away.
A time to rend and a time to sew. A time to keep silence and a time to speak.
A time to love, and a time to hate; a time of war and a time of peace"

***

New Books

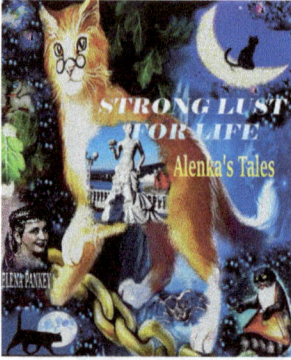

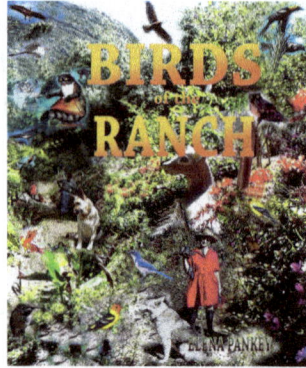

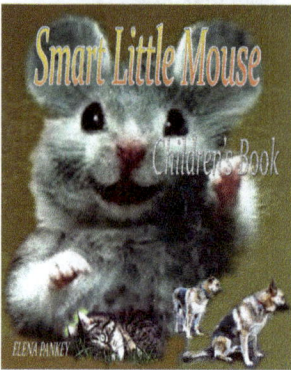

***

Rights Reserved